M000025449

This Journal Belongs to:

ELLA RIDDER

STRAIGHT TALK JOURNALS

This book is copyright protected. Please do not reproduce in either electronic means or in printed format except for your explicit personal use. This means that copying this book is prohibited and not allowed without permission from the author. All Rights Reserved

STRAIGHT TALK JOURNALS

Time to visit Amazon to order your next book. If you found this book useful we hope you will share that by leaving a review on Amazon.

45469650R00060

Made in the USA
Middletown, DE
16 May 2019